TWIN FLAME SURVIVAL KIT

A Guide for the Soul That Refuses to Forget

GRACE BREWSTER

Copyright © 2025 Grace Brewster
All rights reserved.

No part of this book may be reproduced, distributed, or transmitted in any form or by any means, including photocopying, recording, or other electronic or mechanical methods, without the prior written permission of the publisher, except in the case of brief quotations embodied in critical reviews and certain other noncommercial uses permitted by copyright law.

For permission requests, contact:

Email: gracebrewster@telus.net
Facebook: Grace Brewster Author
Instagram @cosmiclovethebook

ISBN: 978-1-0696945-9-1
First Edition 2025

Disclaimer: This book is intended for personal reflection and inspiration. It does not replace professional advice or therapy.

Dedication

For everyone walking through the fire of twin flame awakening. May these pages remind you that love never leaves, it only transforms.

Acknowledgments

To every soul who met themselves in another and dared to keep loving.

To those who walked through fire, silence, and surrender, and still chose compassion over fear.

This book was born from real connection, from the ache and beauty of remembering who we truly are. Thank you to the one who mirrored me most, the reflection that started it all.

And to the unseen Council, guides, and higher selves that whispered when I was ready to listen.

To my friends, both on Earth and beyond, thank you for walking beside me through each chapter of remembering.

May this book bring peace to those still searching, and courage to those ready to awaken.

Table of Contents

Part I The Awakening

1. What Just Happened?
2. Why This Feels Cosmic
3. The Runner & Chaser Dance
4. Twin Flame Myths vs. Reality
5. What to Do When They Vanish
6. Surviving Social Media & Synchronicity Overload
7. Surviving the Silence

Part II   The Healing Integration

8. The Mirror Phase
9. When the Mirror Hurts
10. Emotional Detox & The Soul Purge
11. Boundaries Are Spiritual Too
12. Releasing the Obsession
13. Energetic Cold-Cutting vs. Energetic Harmony
14. The Runners & the Chaser Dynamic
15. Surrender vs. Giving Up
16. The Mirror of Mission
17. The Karmic Intermission
18. The Silence Portal
19. Energetic Overlaps & Phantom Touches
20. When You Feel Their Pain

21. The Magnetic Pull & The Dance Resistance
22. Soul Maturity & the End of Chasing

Part III The Mission & Expansion

23. The Mission Doesn't Wait
24. Merging with Higher Aspects & Dimensional You's
25. Spiritual Readiness & The Mission Frequency

Part IV Closing Section

The Illusion of Waiting
When the Other Twin Isn't Ready
Twin Flame Truths — A Survival Kit in One-Liners
You Are Not Chasing Them
Epilogue

Preface

This book found you for a reason.

Maybe you searched for answers that logic couldn't explain. Maybe you met someone who awakened something ancient inside you, a recognition too deep for words, too impossible to ignore.

If so, I understand. I lived it too.

Twin Flame Survival Kit isn't a manual about finding your other half. It's a companion for remembering your wholeness after love rearranges everything you thought you knew.

The pages that follow were written in real time, between expansion and heartbreak, silence and revelation. They are lessons gathered from living the paradox: feeling infinite love inside a very human body.

Take what resonates and leave the rest. Each chapter is meant to meet you where you are, whether you're aching, healing, or simply curious.

You don't have to believe in twin flames or cosmic contracts. You only have to believe that love transforms us, and that transformation is sacred.

So breathe.

Read slowly.

Let the words remind you that you are not broken, only becoming. And when you're ready, step into the pages as you would into light, not to escape the world, but to see it more clearly.

From the Author's Heart

This book was written for those who found a connection that changed everything. The kind that feels cosmic, timeless, and impossible to ignore.

It's not about chasing love or trying to fix another person. It's about understanding why your soul chose this experience and how to stay centered in your own light while walking through it.

Every twin flame story is unique, yet the awakening it brings is universal.

You are not losing your mind, you are meeting yourself through another soul.

May these words serve as both comfort and compass, reminding you that separation is only a chapter, not the ending. You are both teacher and student in this sacred mirror.

Take what resonates, leave what doesn't, and let these pages remind you that you were never meant to break; you were meant to remember.

The Nature of Flame

A flame isn't destruction — it's expression.

It's what happens when energy remembers it was never meant to stay still.

Flame is movement, warmth, and light, all trying to find form.

When two flames meet, they don't compete; they rise together.

The current between them can light the world or burn through everything false.

To survive the fire is to learn its rhythm,
to breathe with it, to listen, and to let yourself glow without losing who you are.

PART I

The Awakening

Chapter 1: What Just Happened?

You didn't see it coming.

One moment, you were living your life: coffee, emails, small talk, and the next, boom! There they were. It might have been a look across a room, a conversation that started too easily, or even a completely ordinary moment, except it wasn't.

Something in you stopped, turned, and stared. Your body might not have recognized them, but your soul... your soul was already halfway through saying, Oh. It's you.

The Soul Recognition "Click"

There's no universal script for meeting a twin flame, but there's often one common denominator: it feels like remembering, not discovering. It's not getting to know them; it's catching up with someone you've known forever. And it's not always romantic in the beginning. Some twins meet and feel instant chemistry. Others feel instant peace. And some? They feel like they've just locked eyes with their favorite sparring partner from a past life and can't decide whether to hug them or run.

The connection is intense, but it's not just about the person. It's about what your soul recognizes: a shared frequency, a mirrored essence, a piece of home standing in front of you.

Why It Feels Like Lightning in Your Nervous System

When you meet your twin flame, your energy field reacts first, long before your mind catches up.

This can look and feel like:

- Your heart racing for "no reason"
- A magnetic pull toward them, even if you just met
- Unusual calm, like you can breathe differently in their presence
- Or the opposite: anxiety that feels cosmic in scale

The reason? Your soul is waking up to a connection that's existed across lifetimes. It's like finding a bookmark in the middle of a book you didn't know you were reading, and suddenly remembering the whole plot.

The Plot Twist No One Warns You About

Here's the part the internet often skips: meeting your twin flame is not the end of the story; it's the starting gun.

And sometimes, instead of running side-by-side into a glorious sunset, one of you runs... away. This is where the survival kit comes in, because the initial meeting is just the spark.

What follows is a series of shifts, tests, and emotional earthquakes designed to push both of you toward growth , together or apart.

Early-Stage Side Effects

In the days or weeks after meeting, you might notice:

- Energy overload — feeling physically wired or drained for no apparent reason
- Synchronicity storms — angel numbers, repeated words, shared dreams, songs that follow you
- Identity shake-ups — suddenly questioning your life choices, career, or relationships
- Emotional extremes — swinging between euphoria and grief in record time

And here's a bonus one:

- The Weird Brain Loop — replaying everything they said, trying to decode it like a sacred text ("When she said she liked my sweater... was that a sign??")

These aren't random. They're signs that your connection has flipped a switch inside you, and your system is recalibrating.

The First Rule of Twin Flame Survival

The connection is real.
The feelings are real.
But you're still a human living a human life.

Which means you need both:
- Space to honor what's happening on a soul level
- Tools to keep your feet on the ground while your heart is in the stars

This is the balance we're going to build in the chapters ahead.
Not a "how to win them back" manual.
Not a "how to sever the bond" guide.

But a survival kit — emotional, spiritual, and sometimes humorous, to help you navigate the intensity without losing yourself in the process.

Because here's the truth:

Your twin flame journey is as much about you as it is about them. And while the connection might feel fated, how you handle it? That's free will. That's where your power is.

The Cosmic "Oh No" Moment

People romanticize twin flame meetings as the start of a fairytale. Let's get real: sometimes it's more like the start of a complicated group project with the Universe as the supervisor and zero instructions given. Because here's the twist, meeting your twin flame is not the end. It's the starting gun. And sometimes, instead of running together into the sunset, one of you runs away. That's when the real work starts.

Chapter 2: Why This Feels Cosmic (and Why It Can Turn Your Life Upside Down)

So you've met them. You've felt the click. And now you're wondering why this connection feels like it exists on some other frequency entirely; one that ignores logic, time zones, and occasionally, your ability to function like a normal human.

Here's the short version: it's because it is **cosmic**.

This isn't "just chemistry." It's not "just fate." It's the intersection of a soul contract, energetic recognition, and a mutual activation you couldn't switch off even if you tried. And while that might sound beautiful (and it is), it's also why twin flames can send your life into a delightful, terrifying spin.

The "Bigger Than Me" Feeling

From the moment you connect, there's often an unshakable undercurrent: this is not just about us.

It's like the relationship is playing out on two levels at once:

- The human level — the texts, the laughs, the eye contact, the silence, the misunderstandings.
- The soul level — dreams, telepathic flashes, shared emotional waves, and energy exchanges that feel as tangible as touch.

That second level is what makes this feel bigger than life. It's also the part that will demand the most from you, because when your soul is involved, there's no such thing as "casual."

Why It's So Intense

Twin flames act as mirrors for each other's highest potential and deepest wounds.

When you see them, and when they see you, it's like someone just cleaned the glass on your soul's reflection. All the beauty, all the flaws, all the shadow, all the light... it's right there.

The reason this can turn your life upside down is simple: Your soul isn't here to stay comfortable. It's here to grow. And growth, especially at the speed a twin flame triggers, can feel like both a blessing and a demolition project.

Mini-Story: The Unwanted Spotlight

A friend once described meeting her twin flame as "being called on stage in front of a crowd when you're still in your pajamas." That's exactly what it's like, there's no hiding.

The connection will shine a light on parts of yourself you've been ignoring, avoiding, or straight-up pretending didn't exist.

For me, it was my avoidance of vulnerability. I thought I was open. Turns out, I was "open" in the same way a drawbridge is. Sure, I let people in... but only after I was certain the coast was clear.

With a twin flame, there is no coast being clear. They're already inside the gates, asking questions, looking around, and making themselves at home.

The Cosmic Contract

If you believe in pre-birth agreements, and many twin flames do, then this connection is part of a contract you both agreed to before you incarnated.

The contract isn't about possession or obligation.

It's about activation.

You agreed to meet so you could:
- Wake each other up (often abruptly)
- Remind each other of who you really are
- Catalyze each other into your soul's mission faster than you would have gone alone

But here's the tricky part:

Just because the contract exists doesn't mean the human side of either of you will cooperate right away. Free will is always in play, and that's where the turbulence begins.

Why It Feels Like Losing Control

Most relationships operate within the boundaries you set. Twin flame connections? They often don't care about those boundaries.

You might experience:
- A sudden reevaluation of your current relationship or life path
- A magnetic pull toward this person that makes no rational sense
- Emotional highs and lows that feel disproportionate to the circumstances
- Difficulty focusing on anything unrelated to the connection

It's not obsession — it's resonance. Your entire system is responding to a frequency it's known before, and that's hard to file under "normal life."

The Push-Pull Paradox

Here's where the infamous runner/chaser pattern sneaks in.

One twin feels the connection and leans in. The other feels it and panics, pulling away.

This isn't always because they don't care. Often, it's because the energy is overwhelming, like touching a hot stove.

It's too much, too soon, and the instinct is to retreat until it feels safe again.

Understanding this early can save you a lot of hurt. It's not personal rejection, it's self-preservation at a soul level.

The Emotional Earthquake

Think of meeting your twin flame like an earthquake that cracks the foundation of your old life. It doesn't destroy everything, but it will expose the parts of your structure that need repair.

For some, that means ending relationships that no longer align. For others, it means changing careers, moving, or rethinking your priorities entirely. And for many, it means diving headfirst into healing work they've been putting off for years.

Humor Is Your Lifeline

It might seem strange to laugh in the middle of something so life-altering, but humor is one of your best survival tools.

Laugh when they message you about a dream you also had.

Laugh when the same song follows you both for a week.

Laugh when you see their birthday on three different license plates in the same day.

The connection is serious, but you don't have to be solemn to honor it.

Your Survival Mindset for This Stage

Here's what to remember as you navigate this "cosmic earthquake" stage:
- You are not losing your mind (even if it feels like it some days).
- The intensity is part of the purpose; it accelerates your growth.
- You don't have to understand it all right now.
- Keep a sense of humor; it's not disrespect — it's oxygen.

This stage will shake you. It will stretch you. It will demand more of you than you thought you could give. But it will also give you glimpses of your own soul in ways nothing else can. And once you've seen yourself like that? You can't unseen it.

This stage will shake you.

It will stretch you.

It will demand more of you than you thought you could give.

But it will also give you glimpses of your own soul in ways nothing else can.

And once you've seen yourself like that? You can't unseen it.

Chapter 3: The Runner & Chaser Dance (Understanding the Push-Pull Without Losing Your Mind)

If twin flames came with a warning label, it would be this:

CAUTION: May cause sudden urges to run away or chase without warning.

This is the infamous runner/chaser dynamic. It's the part of the twin flame journey that drives people absolutely mad, and for good reason.

One moment, you're in deep connection, finishing each other's sentences. The next, one of you is pulling away like the floor just turned to lava.

If you're in the chaser role, it feels like abandonment.
If you're in the runner role, it feels like survival.
If you've been in both roles (and many twins swap at some point), you know neither is particularly fun.

What's Really Happening Here?

Here's the spiritual truth: the runner/chaser dance isn't about rejection or superiority. It's about emotional regulation in the face of an overwhelming connection.

When one twin feels the energy is too much — too intense, too vulnerable, too fast — the instinct is to create space.

This isn't always conscious. Sometimes the runner doesn't even understand why they're pulling back, only that it feels like self-preservation.

The chaser, on the other hand, feels the connection and wants to close the gap. They sense the pull-away as loss and respond by leaning in harder. Which only makes the runner want to create more distance. And so the loop begins.

Why It Hurts So Much

The runner/chaser dynamic triggers abandonment wounds and fear of loss like nothing else.

If you've ever had someone you love disappear emotionally or physically, this will bring those old wounds right to the surface.

On the flip side, if you've ever felt smothered, trapped, or terrified of losing yourself in a relationship, being on the receiving end of the chase will bring those fears up fast.

This is why the dance is so painful; it's not just about this relationship. It's pulling up all the unfinished business you have around intimacy, trust, and self-worth.

Mini-Story: The Disappearing Act

I once went from daily conversations with my twin to… nothing. No calls, no texts, no "I need space" message. Just silence. At first, I thought something terrible had happened. Then I saw her post a photo from a weekend trip — smiling, carefree, living her life like I didn't exist.

It was brutal. But here's the thing: her distance wasn't about me not mattering. It was about her needing to process the intensity of what we had.

And as much as it stung, that space eventually gave me the room to see how much I'd been outsourcing my happiness to the connection.

The Truth About Roles

One important thing to know: runner and chaser are roles, not identities.

You are not "the runner" forever, and you are not "the chaser" forever. The roles can shift depending on where you both are emotionally and spiritually.

And here's the plot twist:

Sometimes the person who appears to be the runner is actually chasing energetically, just not in obvious ways.

And sometimes the chaser is also running, running from their own healing work by focusing on the other person.

Why the Dance Exists

The runner/chaser dynamic exists for one main reason: to force both of you to grow individually before you can grow together.

- The runner learns to face their fears around intimacy and vulnerability.
- The chaser learns to stop outsourcing their self-worth and to release control.
-

It's not punishment — it's preparation.

How to Survive It Without Losing Your Mind

If you're the chaser right now:

- Stop literal chasing. Give them the space they think they need, even if it feels like the opposite of what you want.
- Anchor yourself. Redirect the energy you're sending toward them into your own healing, creativity, and self-care.
- Detach without disconnecting. You can still hold love for them without monitoring their every move.

If you're the runner right now:

1. Communicate if possible. Even a simple "I need space to process" is kinder than silence.
2. Ask yourself what you're really afraid of. Is it them, or the parts of yourself they're reflecting back?
3. Know that running delays the inevitable. Whatever you're avoiding will still be there when you stop.

Humor Helps (Again)

It might not feel funny in the middle of it, but humor can release the tension. One friend told me she used to joke with her twin flame: "Okay, so are you running clockwise or counterclockwise today? I need to plan my cardio."

It didn't solve the dynamic, but it reminded them that they were still on the same team, even if they were on opposite sides of the room.

The Long View

Most twins don't stay stuck in the runner/chaser stage forever.

It's a phase, and like all phases, it will shift. The key is to use it as a mirror instead of a weapon. Instead of asking, "How do I get them to stop running?" ask, "What is this showing me about myself?"

And remember: your twin flame journey isn't just about reunion. It's about becoming the most aligned version of yourself, whether they're standing next to you or not.

Chapter 4: Twin Flame Myths vs. Reality

The internet loves to romanticize twin flames.

According to some posts, your twin flame is supposed to:
- Show up on a white horse
- Read your mind perfectly
- Never trigger you
- Merge into one blissful soul-hug and live happily ever after

If you've read those posts and are now staring at your very human, very imperfect connection wondering, Did I get the wrong twin?

Let's clear something up:

Most of what you've read online is myth. Real twin flame connections are deeper, messier, and far more transformative than any sugar-coated listicle will tell you.

Myth #1 Twin Flames Are Always Romantic

Reality: While many twin flames experience romantic love, it's not the only way the connection plays out. Some twin flames meet as friends, collaborators, or even family members. The core of the connection isn't about romance, it's about soul recognition and mutual growth. Romance can be part of it, but it's not the defining factor. If it's not romantic, it doesn't mean it's not real.

Myth #2 You'll Be Together Forever Once You Meet

Reality: Meeting your twin flame is the beginning of a journey, not the final chapter. You might have periods of deep closeness followed by long stretches of distance. You might spend years apart, growing individually before reconnecting .

The connection doesn't disappear in separation, but the human relationship might need space to evolve before it can be sustained.

Myth #3 Twin Flames Never Hurt Each Other

Reality: The connection itself isn't hurtful, but the triggers it activates can be. Your twin flame will reflect your deepest wounds back to you, and you'll do the same for them. This mirroring can be uncomfortable, frustrating, and yes, painful at times. It's not intentional cruelty, but it's an accelerated growth process. But it can feel raw until you understand what's happening.

Myth #4 The Signs Will Always Be Positive

Reality: Synchronicities are a big part of twin flame connections, but they're not always sweet, dreamy, or reassuring. Sometimes the signs push you to face uncomfortable truths. Sometimes they show you what needs to change, not what you want to hear.

Seeing their name everywhere doesn't always mean "send them a message." It can mean "heal the part of you that can't let go."

Myth #5 You Must Wait for Them to Awaken

Reality: The journey is as much about your growth as it is about theirs. If you spend all your energy waiting for them to "catch up," you stall your own progress.

The healthiest approach is to keep moving forward, trust that the connection remains, and allow their awakening to happen in its own timing. Or not at all.

Mini-Story: The Reality Check

I once read a blog post that said, "When you meet your twin flame, you'll never doubt the connection." I believed that... until I didn't. When my twin pulled away for the first time, I questioned everything — was it real? Was I imagining it? Did I misread the signs?

What I learned was this: doubt isn't proof the connection is fake. It's proof that you're human. Even the strongest soul connections can feel unclear when you're in the middle of the storm.

Why Myths Can Be Harmful

When you cling to unrealistic expectations, you set yourself up for constant disappointment. If you think your twin flame should never challenge you, you'll panic the moment conflict arises. If you believe you're supposed to be together right now, you might miss the growth available in separation.

Myths turn a living, evolving soul bond into a checklist, and twin flames don't fit in checklists.

Your Reality-Based Survival Mindset

Here's what's actually true:

- The connection is real whether you're together or apart
- Growth can be uncomfortable but it's the point of the journey
- You can love them and still set boundaries
- You are allowed to focus on your life without abandoning the connection

When you release the myths, you give yourself permission to experience the connection as it is, and not as you think it "should" be.

Chapter 5: What to Do When They Vanish (Staying Sane in No Contact)

One of the hardest parts of the twin flame journey is this:
One moment, they're here — present, warm, and fully engaged. The next, it's as if they've been swallowed by the Bermuda Triangle of Communication.

No calls. No texts. No "I just need space" heads-up. Just… gone.
If you've been on the receiving end of this, you know the cocktail of emotions that follows:
- Confusion (Did I do something wrong?)
- Hurt (Why would they just disappear?)
- Panic (Are they okay?)
- Obsession (Check phone. Repeat. Check again.)

Why Twin Flames Disappear

The sudden silence isn't always about you personally. In many cases, your twin flame steps back because the connection has triggered deep emotional or spiritual work they're not ready to face in your presence.

Some possible reasons:

- Overwhelm — The intensity of the connection feels like too much to process all at once.
- Fear of Vulnerability — They see themselves too clearly through you and it scares them.

- Old Wounds — Abandonment, rejection, or commitment fears resurface.
- Life Chaos — External factors (work, family, personal issues) demand their focus.

Knowing this doesn't take away the sting, but it helps you understand that disappearing is often about their inner process, not a verdict on your worth.

The Danger of Chasing in This Phase

When your twin disappears, the instinct to close the gap can be overwhelming. You want to call. Text. Show up at their favorite coffee shop "by accident."

Here's the problem: chasing during no contact usually has the opposite effect you want.

Instead of reassuring them, it increases their need for space. Think of it like trying to hold onto a bird: the tighter you grip, the more it struggles to escape.

What You Can Do Instead

Step 1 Ground Yourself
- Breathe deeply: in for 4, hold for 4, out for 6. Repeat until your nervous system settles.
- Place your hands on your heart and remind yourself: I am safe, I am loved, I am whole.

Step 2. Limit Triggers
- Mute their social media updates for now. No more spiraling over who liked their post.
- Move your phone across the room when you sleep. Nighttime overthinking is a trap.
-

Step 3 Reclaim Your Energy
- Channel your focus into creative projects, hobbies, or physical movement.
- Spend time with supportive friends who won't feed the obsession.

Step 4: Strengthen Your Own Connection

- Meditate or journal about your feelings, not about what they're doing, but about what this brings up in you.
- Remind yourself that the soul bond remains whether or not there's current contact.

Mini-Story: The 21-Day Reset

After my twin disappeared for the first time, I went into full spiral mode, until a friend challenged me to a "21-Day No Twin Check" rule.
No stalking social media.
No rereading old messages.
No playing "our" songs on repeat like a soundtrack for my heartbreak.

The first few days were rough. But by day seven, I noticed I was sleeping better. By day fourteen, my mood was lighter. By day twenty-one, I remembered I actually liked my own company.

And here's the kicker: she messaged me the day after my reset ended. I didn't "manifest" her back, I just stopped drowning in the waiting.

Why Giving Space Works

Space allows both of you to:
- Integrate the lessons and triggers from your last interaction
- Process emotions without pressure
- Reconnect from a place of choice rather than fear

Think of separation not as a wall, but as a reset button. You're still connected — you're just recalibrating.

Your Survival Mindset in No Contact

- This phase is temporary, but your self-respect lasts forever.
- You can love them without chasing them.
- Space doesn't mean absence on a soul level.
- The more you stabilize yourself, the more stable the connection can become in the future.

Chapter 6: Surviving Social Media & Synchronicity Overload

Here's the thing no one warns you about when you meet your twin flame:

You don't just think about them; the whole universe seems to think about them with you. Everywhere you turn, there they are.
Not in person, but in signs.
Songs.
Repeating numbers.
 "Random" posts that feel like secret messages from the cosmos.
And then there's social media — the modern-day psychic torture chamber.

The Double-Edged Sword of Social Media

For twin flames in any stage of the journey, social media can be both a comfort and a trigger. You see a post from them and your heart leaps... only to sink seconds later because they're smiling with someone else, or posting from a place you weren't invited to. Or maybe you overanalyze every emoji they use, every playlist they share, every cryptic quote they post at 2 a.m.

Spoiler alert:
This way lies madness.

The Synchronicity Storm

Meanwhile, the Universe is on its own campaign to keep you awake at night.
- Repeating numbers: 11:11, 2:22, 4:44 — every clock, every receipt, every street sign.
- Shared songs: The one you once heard together suddenly plays in the middle of a random grocery run.
- Dream appearances: You wake up convinced you just had a conversation with them.
- Weird "chance" encounters: You keep running into people with their name, same birthday, or who bring them up out of nowhere.

It's beautiful and maddening all at once.

The Problem with Over-Focusing on Signs

Signs are meant to guide and encourage you, not chain you to constant emotional whiplash.

Here's the thing: if you over-attach to them, you risk missing the reason they're showing up. Often, the message is less about "look at them" and more about "look at what this is awakening in you."

Your Social Media Survival Plan

1. Mute with Love

Muting them doesn't mean you're cutting the cord. It means you're protecting your nervous system from overload.

2. Stop the Compare Game

Their feed is not their full reality. You're seeing highlight reels, not their entire emotional landscape.

3. Replace the Scroll

If you feel the urge to check their profile, replace it with something nourishing like watch a funny video, read a chapter of a book, go outside for five minutes.

Your Synchronicity Sanity Guide

Step 1. Thank the Sign, Then Release It
When a synchronicity happens, acknowledge it out loud or in your journal, then let it go.

This keeps you in gratitude without spiraling into obsession.

Step 2 . Ask for Clarity

If a sign keeps repeating, meditate or journal on what it means for you, not just for the connection.

Step 3. Balance Signs with Action

Signs are powerful, but they're not a substitute for building your own life and mission.

When the Signs Lead to Purpose

For some twin flames, and I count myself here, the signs didn't just keep me thinking about them. They kept nudging me toward my mission.

The connection became a catalyst. The visions, the numbers, the dreams — they didn't just point me toward her. They pointed me toward me.

Toward my writing. Toward my awakening. Toward remembering why I even came here in the first place.

And that's the thing: sometimes the twin flame isn't meant to be your forever partner in the 3D. Sometimes they're the spark that lights the torch you carry forward. If the signs are guiding you toward your mission, follow them. That's where the real magic is.

Quick Exercise: Sign Reframe

Next time you see a repeating number, a song, or a "coincidence" connected to them, ask:
- What's happening in my life right now that this could be pointing to?
- What action can I take today that honors both this sign and my personal growth?

The point isn't to ignore the connection, it's to make sure it's fueling you instead of draining you.

Chapter 7: Surviving the Silence (When They Pull Away)

There comes a point in every twin flame journey when the energy shifts. Messages stop. The warmth fades. The universe, once loud with signs, goes eerily quiet.

You check your phone, scroll their feed, look for synchronicities that will explain it, but the silence itself is the message.

Here's what no one tells you:

Silence is not rejection. It's spiritual surgery.

When they pull away, the universe isn't punishing you — it's realigning both of you. The distance isn't emptiness; it's sacred space being created for healing that can't happen when you're tangled in each other's energy. The human part of you will want to chase. The soul part of you already knows better.

The Problem with Taking Silence Personally

Your twin's silence triggers every wound of abandonment you've ever carried, not because they caused it, but because they activated it.

Their withdrawal is not a wall; it's a mirror.

When you start asking, "Why did they stop talking to me?" try shifting it to "What in me is afraid of being alone?" That's where your real healing begins.

Your Emotional Survival Plan

1. Don't fill the silence.
Resist the urge to reach out, post, or perform to get their attention. Let the quiet be loud enough to hear your own heartbeat again.
2. Let energy speak before words.
If you feel their presence, talk to their higher self instead of their phone. The soul always answers, even when the person doesn't.
3. Turn silence into sanctuary.
Use this time to rebuild your inner world. Journal, walk, create. The same energy that once chased them can now fuel your expansion.

When Silence Becomes Communication

Sometimes the silence is saying,
"I need to remember who I am without you."

Other times, it's whispering,
"You've grown beyond needing my validation."

Either way, you're both being guided to evolve.

The truth is: if the bond is real, silence never severs it. It only shifts it to a higher frequency, where connection is no longer based on conversation, but on resonance.

Quick Exercise: Turning the Silence into Sound

When the quiet feels heavy, ask yourself:
1. What part of me feels unsafe without their voice?
2. What creative act can I do right now to give that part comfort?
3.

Then do it. Write a page, sing, dance, or even whisper to the stars. Let your own soul make the sound you've been waiting to hear.

PART II

The Healing Integration

Chapter 8: The Mirror Phase (Seeing Yourself in Them)

When you meet your twin flame, you don't just meet another person — you meet yourself in another body. And that reflection is not always comfortable to look at.

They show you the beauty you forgot, and the shadows you've been avoiding. You love them, but what you're really doing is remembering you.

The Reflection Game

Every word, every silence, every reaction, they mirror something unhealed within you. When they withdraw, it mirrors your own fear of abandonment. When they won't open up, it mirrors where you still hold back your truth.

When they love you unconditionally, it mirrors how hard it is to receive love without earning it.

The connection is designed this way, not to punish, but to awaken.

Trigger or Teacher?

In the early stages, you might think, They're hurting me, but as consciousness expands, you see it differently: They're showing me where I've been hurting myself.

That realization shifts everything. The triggers become portals, the pain becomes practice, the reflection becomes revelation.

How to Work with the Mirror

1. Observe before reacting. When they trigger you, pause. Ask, What is this really showing me about me?

2. Don't analyze them, study your reflection. Their behavior is the mirror frame — you are the image.

3. Respond with compassion. The same wound they trigger in you, they carry in another form. You're both learning to love what was once unloved.

When It Feels Too Intense

Mirroring can feel brutal. It's like staring at a version of you you're not ready to face. That's when you take a step back and breathe.

Remember: you don't have to fix what you see, only accept it. Once you do, the reflection softens.

The Mirror Turns Clear

As you heal, the reflection changes. They no longer trigger you in the same way. What once burned now blesses. The connection becomes less about reacting, and more about radiating.

Because when you love your reflection, you no longer need someone else to reflect it.

And that's when the journey truly begins, not chasing the mirror, but embodying the love that made it appear.

Quick Practice: Mirror Gratitude

1. Write down three moments your twin triggered you.
2. Under each, write what that taught you about yourself.
3. End with: Thank you for showing me…
4. Read it aloud. Feel the shift from pain to peace.

Chapter 9: When the Mirror Hurts (Shadow Work & Triggers)

One of the hardest truths about the twin-flame connection is this: they are not only your mirror of love — they're your mirror of pain.

Every time you see them, hear their name, or think about them, the reflection isn't just them. It's you. All the unhealed parts, all the forgotten wounds, all the patterns you swore you were done with.

That's what makes this connection so holy… and so hard.

The Mirror Effect

Your twin doesn't show you what you want to see.
They show you what needs to be seen.
That moment of jealousy, that rush of fear, that ache when they pull away, it's not proof that they're cruel. It's proof that something inside you is still asking to be held.

When you say, "They hurt me," the universe whispers, "They revealed you."

You can't heal what you won't look at, and nothing makes you look faster than a mirror that breathes your name.

The Trigger Isn't Punishment

A trigger is not the universe being mean.
It's an invitation.
It says, "Here's a part of your heart that's still trembling. Bring light here."

So the next time you feel the sting — the rejection, the jealousy, the fear of loss. Pause.
Ask:

1. What is this emotion trying to tell me?
2. Where have I felt this before?
3. What does it need from me now?

You'll start to notice something extraordinary: the moment you stop fighting the trigger, it transforms into guidance.

Your Shadow Work Survival Plan

1. Feel, Don't Fix.
You don't have to rush your healing.
Sit with the discomfort.
Let tears teach you what peace never could.

2. Journal Instead of React.
Write before you text.
Feel before you speak.
Sometimes the most powerful message you can send is the one you never deliver.

3. Love Yourself Louder.
Every time they withdraw, love yourself twice as much.
Every time they reflect your pain, give yourself the compassion you once begged for.

When the Shadow Turns to Light

The gift of this mirror is that it doesn't lie.
It will keep showing you what's unhealed until you finally embrace it.
And when you do, the energy shifts.
The next time you look at them, you'll no longer see pain.
You'll see growth.
You'll see how far you've come.

The twin-flame journey isn't about perfection.
It's about purification; the slow, radiant process of becoming your own light.

Quick Exercise: Mirror Check-In

Look into a mirror and say:
"I forgive myself for everything I projected.
I am willing to see this with love."

Then close your eyes and imagine the reflection glowing back at you, not as their face, but as your healed self smiling.

That's the real union: when the reflection stops hurting and starts humming with peace.

Chapter 10: Emotional Detox & The Soul Purge

You think you've cried all the tears possible, and then another wave hits.
This isn't heartbreak as you once knew it.
It's deeper. It's cellular. It's like your entire being is purging lifetimes of emotion you didn't even know you carried.

It's the soul's detox, and it comes for everyone on this path.

The Purge Begins

The moment your heart cracks open through this connection, the Universe uses it as an entry point to clean everything you've suppressed. Suddenly, anger from childhood resurfaces.

Old fears, forgotten grief, jealousy, and abandonment all rise like ghosts asking to be freed.

You may feel exhausted, emotional, or even physically unwell. It's not regression; it's release.

You're not breaking down — you're breaking open.

What's Really Happening

Your energy field is reorganizing.
The love this connection activates is so high-frequency that anything unaligned with it must surface to be cleared. It's like light flooding a dusty room; everything hidden becomes visible.

That visibility is healing.

You can't clean what you refuse to see.

The Cleansing Process

1. Let the tears come.
Tears are sacred. They are water remembering how to flow again.

2. Ground daily.
Your body is your stabilizer. Walk, breathe, eat nourishing foods, touch the Earth.

3. Rest more than usual.
Upgrades need integration time. Don't fight fatigue, honor it.

4. Don't try to "positive-think" your way through it.
You can't bypass emotions with affirmations. You have to feel to heal.

The Emotional Triggers

The detox will be triggered by memories, songs, smells, messages, even dreams.

You'll think you're fine, and suddenly, you're crying over a line in a movie.

It's okay. Nothing is wrong with you.

That's your soul wringing out energy that's no longer needed.

When It Finally Eases

One day, the heaviness lifts.
The air feels lighter.

You wake up and realize you can think of them without pain.
The body that once trembled now feels grounded.

The eyes that once burned from crying now see clearly.
That's the sign: you've moved from purging to peace.

Your heart didn't close; it expanded.
You've made space for the next phase — wholeness.

Quick Practice: The Energy Flush

1. Sit or lie down.
2. Breathe deeply into your belly.
3. Imagine a waterfall of golden-white light pouring through your crown, washing through your body.
4. Whisper: I release all that no longer serves love.
5. Stay until you feel calm or lighter.

The cleansing of the soul isn't intended as a penalty; it's meant for readiness. Because only an emptied vessel can hold divine love without breaking.

Chapter 11: Boundaries Are Spiritual Too (Learning that love without limits becomes chaos. How to protect your peace)

Unconditional love doesn't mean unconditional access.
There's a difference between being open-hearted
and being unguarded.

On the twin flame path,
you learn that energy is sacred currency,
and not everyone is meant to spend it freely.

When you give and give without balance,
even love can become distortion.
What begins as compassion
can quietly turn into depletion.

Boundaries aren't walls.
They're alignment tools.

They keep your energy clear enough
to serve its higher purpose.
They teach others how to meet you
with respect and awareness.

They remind the universe
that your love has structure —
that even the divine operates
within sacred order.

A boundary says:
"I love you, but I love myself too."
"I can hold space for your pain,
but I can't hold it for you."
"I will always meet you with truth,
but not at the cost of my peace."

The most spiritual thing you can sometimes do
is step back.

To protect your energy
is to protect your mission.

To say no with love
is to say yes to your higher self.

Remember —
the flame burns brightest
when it has air to breathe.

Reflection:

Where am I giving too much of myself
in the name of love?
What does peace feel like in my body,
and how can I choose it more often?

Chapter 12: Releasing the Obsession Loop

You wake up thinking of them.
You go to sleep thinking of them.
Even your dreams have joined the mission.

It's not madness — it's energy overflow.
Your system is learning how to contain something infinite inside a finite human body.

When Love Turns into a Loop

Obsession happens when the energy of connection gets trapped in the mind instead of flowing through the heart.

You keep replaying every moment, every word, every sign — like trying to decode a message that's already been delivered.

You're not actually addicted to the person.
You're addicted to the feeling they awaken.

The moment you met them, a circuit opened.
Now your soul is learning how to regulate that current without short-circuiting.

The Brain vs. The Soul

Your brain wants logic: What does this mean? Will they come back?
Your soul only wants experience: Feel this, integrate this, evolve through this.

The two fight for control — the brain builds stories; the soul builds wisdom.
Obsession fades when you stop feeding the story and start listening to the wisdom.

Breaking the Loop

1. Interrupt the thought spiral.
When your mind starts looping, pause and name it: This is the loop.
Breathe deeply into your belly.
Awareness breaks pattern.

2. Move the energy.
Walk, dance, paint, write, cook — do anything physical or creative.
The energy must flow out of the head and into the body.

3. Reclaim your timeline.
Obsession steals presence.
Start small: a walk without checking your phone, a meal without mental dialogue.
Each moment reclaimed returns you to your own orbit.

4. Don't punish yourself for still thinking of them.
Obsession dissolves through love, not shame.
You can't heal by hating your humanness.

The Transformation of Focus

When the loop quiets, something magical happens — you rediscover space.

You begin hearing your own voice again.

Ideas return. Joy returns. Life starts expanding around you, not revolving around them.

And that's when the energy of love matures from attachment to awareness.

The Freedom You Forgot

You were never meant to chase.
You were meant to create.
The obsession was the cocoon, now you're remembering your wings.

Once you break the loop, you don't lose them, you simply stop orbiting them.

And that's how the Universe knows you're ready for the next phase: creation, not fixation.

Quick Practice: The Flame Reset

- Close your eyes and imagine two flames — one theirs, one yours.
- See where they intertwine too tightly.
- Gently separate them, letting each stand strong on its own.
- Whisper: We burn in harmony, not dependency.

When you open your eyes, feel how much lighter it is to love freely.

Chapter 13: Energetic Cord-Cutting vs. Energetic Harmony

There's a lot of confusion about cords.
People say, "Cut the cord, detach, move on."
But how do you cut something that's made of light?
How do you undo what was woven before time?

Here's the truth: you can't sever energy that was created in love.
But you can clean it.
You can balance it.
You can choose harmony over obsession.

The Myth of Cutting Cords

Cutting sounds final — like slamming a door.
But energy doesn't work like that.
It moves in waves.
Every thought, every emotion, every memory you send toward them is a current.
When you're angry, it spikes.
When you're peaceful, it settles.

So instead of cutting cords, think of tuning frequencies.
You're not deleting the connection — you're changing the channel.

From Attachment to Alignment

Attachment says, "I need them to complete me."
Alignment says, "I am complete, and the connection amplifies my light."

When you shift from attachment to alignment, the cord transforms.
It stops draining you and starts sustaining you.

You'll still feel their energy, but softer, calmer, like background music instead of thunder.

The Energetic Hygiene Routine

1. Clear Daily.

Imagine golden light running through your body like water through a crystal.
Breathe in peace, breathe out residue.
This isn't to erase them, it's to release what isn't yours.

2. Return to Sender (with Love).

If you sense heavy emotion that doesn't belong to you, say quietly:
"I send back all energy that isn't mine, wrapped in love and light."
No anger. No blame. Just release.

3. Reclaim Your Center.
Touch your heart and remind yourself:
"My energy is my home."
Because sometimes the real healing isn't about
detaching — it's about remembering where you live.

When Harmony Arrives

One day you'll realize the cord isn't choking you anymore.
You'll think of them and feel peace instead of panic.

Their name won't burn; it will bless.
That's when the connection has matured.

It's not gone; it's become sacred neutrality.
In that space, both souls can breathe freely, still linked, but no longer bound.

That is energetic harmony.
That is freedom.

Quick Exercise: The Golden Thread

1. Sit quietly.
2. Visualize a golden thread connecting your heart to theirs.
3. See it pulsing gently, not pulling.
4. Whisper: "May this connection serve our highest good only."
5. Then imagine the golden thread widening into light that flows through both of you and out into the cosmos, dissolving any imbalance, leaving only love.

Chapter 14: The Runner and the Chaser Dynamic

If there's one pattern every twin flame seems to face, it's this:
One runs.
One chases.
And it feels like hell.

You've probably asked yourself: Why can't we both just stop?
Here's why: the runner/chaser dynamic isn't about punishment.
It's about pressure.
It's the Universe's way of forcing both souls to expand.

Why One Runs

Running isn't always physical.
It's emotional distance.
It's ignoring messages, making excuses, changing plans.
It's a survival reflex that says: "This is too much. I'm not ready to see myself through you."

Behind the runner is fear.
Fear of intimacy.
Fear of reflection.
Fear of the soul's own power.

Why One Chases

Chasing isn't always obvious either.
It's checking their social media.
It's over-explaining, over-texting, over-feeling.
It's a survival reflex that says: "If I can hold onto you, I won't lose myself."

Behind the chaser is fear too.
Fear of abandonment.
Fear of rejection.
Fear that the connection might vanish.

The Hidden Gift

Both roles are mirrors.
The runner's distance forces the chaser to turn inward.

The chaser's intensity forces the runner to face their heart.
No one wins this game; everyone transforms through it.

This is why the dynamic feels like fire — it's burning off what's not real.

Shifting the Dance

You can't make them stop running.
You can only stop chasing.
When you withdraw your chasing energy, the cord rebalances.
Sometimes they return.
Sometimes they don't.
But either way, you return to yourself.

And here's the paradox: the moment you stop chasing, you stop being a chaser.
You become a lighthouse.
You stand. You shine. You send out steady light.
They may run, but they'll always know where the light is.

From Tug-of-War to Parallel Paths

Think of it less as a chase and more as two parallel paths.
You walk yours. They walk theirs.
You meet where the paths naturally cross.
No pulling, no pushing, just convergence at the right time.

This shift changes everything.
You move from need to alignment.

From fear to trust.
From drama to destiny.

Quick Exercise: The Lighthouse Practice

Next time you feel the urge to reach out, pause.
Close your eyes.
Visualize yourself as a lighthouse on a cliff.
Bright. Steady. Silent.
Your twin flame is at sea.

You're not swimming after them; you're shining.
Repeat:

"I do not chase. I do not run. I stand. I shine."

This calms your nervous system and restores your power.
It also gently sends a signal to their soul: the safe harbor is within.

Chapter 15: Surrender vs. Giving Up

Every twin flame journey hits the moment when you whisper to yourself, "I can't do this anymore."
But there's a vast difference between surrender and giving up — one frees you, the other freezes you.

Giving Up

Giving up comes from exhaustion.
It sounds like: "I quit. This was a mistake. I hate this connection."
It feels heavy, bitter, resigned.

When you give up, you shut down your heart to protect it.
The pain stops for a while, but so does the growth.

Surrender

Surrender comes from wisdom.
It sounds like: "I release control. I let this unfold in its own time."
It feels lighter, like unclenching a fist.

Surrender keeps your heart open without letting it bleed.
It stops the drama without stopping the love.

How to Know Which One You're In

- Bitterness = giving up.
- Peace = surrender.
- Fear = giving up.
- Trust = surrender.

This isn't about forcing yourself to "be positive." It's about noticing your energy. You can still surrender while feeling sad, the difference is you're no longer fighting reality.

Your Surrender Survival Plan

1. Name it.

Say out loud: "I choose surrender." Even if your mind resists, your energy will begin to shift.

2. Release the outcome.

Stop trying to guess when or how union will happen. Focus on your healing, your mission, your joy.

3. Keep your heart open.

Surrender doesn't mean shutting them out forever. It means creating space for something higher to enter.

The Paradox of Surrender

The more you let go, the less you lose.
When you stop clinging, the connection stops slipping through your fingers.

Surrender is not the end of the story.
It's the beginning of a new chapter — one where you stand in your power, anchored and radiant, regardless of what your twin chooses.

Quick Exercise: The Open Hands

Close your eyes.
Clench your fists. Feel the tension.
Now slowly open your hands and whisper:

"I release control, but I keep my heart."

Do this whenever you feel yourself spiraling.
It resets your nervous system and gently moves you from giving up into surrender.

Chapter 16: The Mirror of Mission (When Pain Pushes You Into Purpose)

Every twin-flame path eventually asks the same question:
"Now that my heart is shattered open, what will I do with all this light?"

The connection was never only about romance.
It was training. A cosmic internship in empathy, surrender, and unconditional love.

And once you survive the storm, you realize the energy has to go somewhere because awakening without direction feels like static.

When Pain Becomes Fuel

Pain isn't a dead end; it's compressed energy waiting to move.
The moment you stop trying to fix the story and start creating from it, it transforms.

Write. Paint. Teach. Cook. Travel. Build.

Anything that channels the voltage turns agony into architecture.

Your twin might have ignited the fire, but you decide what it lights.

The Shift from Personal to Planetary

At first the mission feels personal: heal, understand, find peace.

Then something inside whispers, "What if my healing could help others too?"

That's when mission activates.

It's not grand or glamorous — it's alignment.

Every act of compassion, every page you write, every truth you speak becomes circuitry for collective healing.

Your Mission Survival Plan

1. Follow what feels alive.
If it expands you, it's part of the mission.
If it drains you, it's part of the old pattern.

2. Detach from their role.
Your twin doesn't have to walk beside you for your mission to move forward.
You're both working for the same Source, just on different shifts.

3. Serve from overflow.
Don't pour from your wounds. Fill yourself first, then let the excess love spill into the world.

When Purpose Finds You

One day you'll notice that thinking of them no longer hurts — it inspires.

You'll realize the mission isn't something you chase; it's what rises naturally when love has nowhere else to go but outward.

The twin flame journey isn't just two souls finding each other.

It's Source finding expression through both.

Quick Exercise: Purpose Pulse

Place your hand over your heart and ask:
"Where does this energy want to flow today?"

Listen for the first impulse: a call, a post, a project, a nap. Then follow it.

That's how mission speaks: quietly, consistently, always through what feels most alive.

Chapter 17: The Karmic Intermission (When Someone Else Appears)

There comes a point in this journey when someone new enters the scene.

They're kind, available, maybe even adorable, and suddenly you're in what I call the karmic intermission.

Don't panic. It doesn't erase the twin connection; it just means the universe has brought in a substitute teacher while your soul partner finishes their homework.

Why the Karmic Appears

Karmic partners show up to balance energies, teach lessons, and remind you that you're still human.

They often mirror what your twin couldn't give you — consistency, affection, presence, because you needed to know how that feels.

Sometimes, they also reflect what you still need to release: control, guilt, the need to fix others.

They're not a punishment. They're a pause button for growth.

The Difference Between Karmic and Twin

- The karmic connection feels comfortable.
- The twin connection feels cosmic.
- Karmic love teaches boundaries.
- Twin love teaches unconditional acceptance.
- Karmic lessons have end dates.
- Twin lessons keep evolving.

Both are important. Without karmic relationships, we'd never learn how to function in 3D reality; without twin flames, we'd never remember the higher one.

Your Karmic Survival Plan

1. Don't compare.
They're not replacements. They're reflections. Each connection serves a different syllabus.

2. Stay honest.
If you feel yourself using someone to fill the twin-shaped silence, pause. That's not love; that's emotional substitution.

3. Take the gift.
Learn what this person came to teach you, then let them go with gratitude when the lesson completes.

When the Curtain Closes

You'll know the karmic chapter is ending when peace replaces passion.

No drama, no guilt, just a quiet knowing: "This served its purpose."

And the next thing you know, you'll catch a new synchronicity from your twin not to restart chaos, but to remind you that all paths are converging again in divine timing.

Quick Exercise: The Gratitude Release

Write this in your journal:

"Thank you for showing me what I needed to see.
I release you with love, and I release myself from needing lessons the hard way."

Say it out loud if you can. You'll feel a lightness right behind the sadness, as the karma untying its final knot.

Journal

Chapter 18: The Silence Portal (When No Contact Becomes Healing)

No contact.

Two words that feel like punishment but are actually protection.

It's the phase no one wants, yet every twin flame eventually meets: the void. The in-between. The quiet where even the Universe seems to whisper, "Don't text."

The Void Isn't Empty

Silence doesn't mean the connection is over. It means your soul is under renovation.

The energy that once bounced between you is now being redirected inward, forcing both twins to face themselves without the distraction of the other's mirror.

You're not being ignored.

You're being prepared.

Why Silence Feels So Loud

Your energy systems have been intertwined, so when communication stops, your body still listens. You might dream of them, feel phantom touches, or sense their mood. It's maddening and magical all at once.

The key is learning not to chase those signals.
Let them drift by like clouds. They're reminders that energy never dies; it simply changes form.

The Hidden Purpose of No Contact

Silence gives space for sovereignty.

It's where codependency dissolves, where both of you rebuild your personal frequency so the next connection can be healthier, lighter, freer.

It's also where your spiritual muscles develop — trust, patience, intuition.

You stop waiting by your phone and start listening to your higher self instead.

Your Silence Survival Plan

1. Treat silence like sacred space.
Light candles, journal, meditate — turn the waiting room into a sanctuary.

2. Stop checking for signs.
The silence isn't a riddle to decode. It's a rest period. You don't check the oven every five minutes while baking; let the energy cook.

3. Speak to their higher self.
When words can't reach them, energy still can. Whisper love through your heart, not your keyboard.

When Silence Becomes Sound

One day, you'll stop feeling the ache and start hearing peace.

That's when you know the silence has done its work.
It hasn't broken the connection; it's refined it.

The portal opens again sometimes through a message, sometimes through a dream, sometimes through a whole new you.

And you'll realize: the silence was never the end.
It was the breath between lifetimes.

Quick Exercise: The Candle Ritual

1. Light a candle and imagine it representing your connection.
2. Sit quietly for 5 minutes.
3. Whisper: "We are safe in the silence."
4. Blow out the flame and visualize both of you surrounded by calm, golden light.

This tells the Universe that you've made peace with the pause, and that peace is what draws the next chapter closer.

Chapter 19: Energetic Overlaps & Phantom Touches

It's not your imagination.

That sudden warmth on your shoulder, that chill down your spine, that heartbeat that isn't yours, these are all echoes of your energetic connection.

When you meet your twin, your frequencies overlap like two merging songs. Even when you're apart, the melody keeps playing, sometimes faint, sometimes loud, but always familiar.

The Physics of Feeling Them

You are both made of energy fields that extend far beyond the body.

When the connection is active, the energy waves ripple through dimensions.

Your soul senses them before your mind understands what's happening.

That's why, in the middle of a quiet evening, your body might respond as if someone invisible just walked through the room.

It's not haunting, it's resonance.

The Gift and the Challenge

Feeling them from afar is a reminder that love is not bound by distance.

But it can also be overwhelming, especially when you're trying to move on.

You think, Why now? Why can I still feel them when I've done everything to let go?

Because the Universe isn't done teaching through that frequency.

You're still learning mastery over your own energy — learning that feeling doesn't always require reacting.

How to Ground Through the Overlap

When you sense their presence, try this:

1. Acknowledge without attachment.
Say silently: I feel you, and I release you with love.

2. Anchor in your body.
Touch something physical — your desk, your clothes, your heart. Feel what's real now.

3. Redirect the current.
Use the energy surge to create — write, paint, walk, dance. Transform the sensation into movement.

Why It Happens More at Night

The veil between dimensions thins when your mind quiets. You relax, your shields drop, and the energetic cords become more noticeable.

It's not a haunting, it's a reminder of unity.

The more you resist it, the stronger it feels.

The more you accept it as natural, the softer it becomes.

The Evolution of Touch

At first, it startles you, an electric charge.

Then it becomes comfort, a subtle pulse.

Eventually, it evolves into neutrality, not the absence of love, but the transcendence of it.

When you reach that stage, you'll understand:

you were never being touched from the outside.

You were remembering how it feels to be whole from the inside.

Quick Practice: Energy Ownership

1. Close your eyes and breathe into your heart.
2. Imagine your energy as golden threads woven within your aura.
3. Whisper: Only my energy belongs in my field.
4. Visualize the threads pulling back into you, sealing with gentle light.

Chapter 20: When You Feel Their Pain

There will be moments when you feel an ache that doesn't belong to you.

A heaviness in your chest, a sudden wave of sadness, tears that arrive without a story.

You check yourself, I'm fine, so why do I feel like I'm falling apart?

That's the mystery of shared energetic empathy when your twin flame's pain crosses through the unseen bridge that connects your fields.

The Bridge of Empathy

This is not punishment.

It's a reminder that energy is language, and you're fluent in theirs.

The emotional current moves both ways; what one resists, the other might process.

It's not always conscious. Sometimes you wake up exhausted because, somewhere in another timezone, they finally cried for the first time in months.

The Difference Between Yours and Theirs

The first key to peace is discernment.

Ask quietly: Is this mine?

If it lifts even slightly when you ask, it's not yours.

Empathy doesn't mean carrying their wounds; it means understanding them.

You're not meant to heal for them, only to witness the energy and release it through compassion, not through suffering.

Turning Pain into Power

Each time you feel their distress, you have a sacred opportunity to transmute.

Breathe it in gently, and on the exhale, imagine sending back pure golden light.

Say: I feel your energy, but I return it to you wrapped in love and peace.

You're not abandoning them; you're honouring sovereignty.

Why It Feels So Personal

Twin flames mirror everything — love, joy, and yes, pain.

You feel it deeply because their lessons echo your own unhealed layers.

Their heartbreak might touch your own. Their loneliness might mirror your forgotten grief.

But awareness breaks the loop.

When you can observe without drowning, you evolve from empath to alchemist.

The Moment of Release

One day, you'll sense their pain again, but this time, your heart will stay open and calm.

You'll breathe in compassion, not panic.

That's when you'll know the bridge has transformed from wire to light.

Their healing no longer destabilizes you; it harmonizes with you.

It's still connection, but now, it's clean.

Quick Practice: The Empath's Reset

1. Place your right hand on your heart.
2. Breathe in through your nose, and exhale through your mouth three times.
3. Say softly: I return all energy that is not mine, with love.
4. Visualize golden light filling every cell.

You'll feel lighter, not because they've changed, but because you've released the need to carry what was never yours to begin with.

Chapter 21: The Magnetic Pull & The Dance of Resistance

No matter how much time passes, no matter how many miles stretch between you, something keeps pulling.

You can feel it when you're calm.

You can feel it when you're done.

It's not obsession.

It's recognition.

Twin flames orbit each other like stars sharing the same gravitational field.

You can walk away, fall silent, date other people, and still, the invisible current hums beneath your life.

It's not punishment; it's design.

That magnetism is the soul's way of saying, "I'm not finished learning from you."

The Push and Pull

One runs. The other waits.

Then the roles switch.

It's not a chase, it's an energetic calibration.

The runner is not cruel; they're overwhelmed.

They feel the same connection but don't have the tools to manage it.

Their retreat gives space for integration for both of you.

The chaser isn't desperate; they're activated.

They feel what's possible and can't understand why the other won't step into it.

But chasing disrupts alignment.

Energy that is meant to harmonize starts to collide.

The Lesson Hidden in the Magnet

When you stop chasing, the polarity begins to balance.
The pull doesn't vanish, it softens.

You start to understand that the purpose was never reunion, but evolution.

That longing in your chest isn't for the person — it's for the part of you they awaken.

The moment you integrate that energy within, the dynamic shifts.

They might return, or not.
Either way, the magnet has done its work.

The Resistance Dance

When your twin resists, don't take it personally.
They're not rejecting you; they're rejecting the reflection.
The mirror can be too bright when they're not ready to see themselves.

Your role is not to convince them to look.
Your role is to keep shining anyway.

When you stand fully in your energy, without pushing, the Universe rebalances the polarity.

They will either rise to meet your frequency or fade into the distance until they're ready.

Both outcomes are love.

The Shift from Pull to Peace

One day, the magnetic ache will turn into a quiet knowing.

The push and pull will dissolve into neutrality.

And when you finally feel that peace, the lesson of resistance is complete.

It's not about having them; it's about becoming whole enough that you don't need to.

The magnetism remains, but it doesn't move you anymore. It simply glows.

Quick Practice: Center of Gravity

1. Sit quietly and imagine a magnetic field around your heart.
2. Feel its pull, then slowly breathe until the pull softens into warmth.
3. Whisper: I am my own gravity. I hold myself in orbit.

Every time you do this, you reclaim another piece of your energy, and the dance becomes less about longing, more about love.

Chapter 22: Soul Maturity & The End of Chasing

There comes a moment when the chase simply stops, not because you gave up, but because your soul grew up.

You wake up one morning and realize you don't need closure, you don't need answers, and you don't need them to come back for you to be whole.

You still feel them, yes.

But now, it no longer hurts — it hums.

The Graduation of Energy

When you meet your twin flame, your soul enrolls in the highest class of emotional evolution.

The syllabus includes unconditional love, patience, surrender, boundaries, and trust.

The final lesson is detachment... not from love, but from control.

You stop chasing because you finally understand:
nothing real can be lost, and nothing forced will ever stay.

The New Kind of Love

Soul maturity brings a new frequency of love — quiet, spacious, and steady.

It's love that doesn't demand.
It blesses from afar.

It smiles when thinking of them, not because they're yours, but because they exist.

This is when the longing transforms into gratitude.
The tears turn into peace.
The story turns into strength.

The Illusion of Losing

You never lose your twin flame.

You lose the version of yourself who thought love meant holding on tightly.

Once that dissolves, what remains is freedom, the kind that lets both souls evolve in their own time, their own way.

When the Journey Becomes the Gift

The most mature stage of the connection is realizing
the purpose was never reunion, it was remembrance.

You didn't meet them to complete you.
You met them to remember what you already are.

Every heartbreak, every silence, every synchronicity, they all refined you.

The fire burned away what wasn't true.
Now, you stand as the distilled essence of love itself.

The Real Victory

You no longer need to chase what's already within you.
That's soul maturity — the quiet power that says,
"I release you, and I love you still."

You walk forward lighter, wiser, more open, not waiting, not yearning, simply being.

And from that space, the Universe aligns everything meant for you, sometimes including them, sometimes something far greater.

Quick Practice: The Release Blessing

1. Close your eyes and hold your hands over your heart.
2. Whisper: Thank you for awakening me. I release you to your highest path.
3. Imagine your energy expanding beyond the story into pure, golden light.

That's the end of chasing, and the beginning of true creation.

PART III

The Mission and Expansion

Chapter 23: The Mission Doesn't Wait (Even If They're Asleep)

Here's one of the hardest truths you'll face on the twin flame path:
Sometimes, the mission clock starts ticking before the other flame is ready.

You might be here with your bags packed — soul codes downloaded, heart open, ready to step into your shared purpose, only to find your counterpart still lost in Earth's distractions, still avoiding the pull, or still tangled in their own karmic webs.

It can feel unfair. It can feel lonely. And it can feel like the whole Universe played a joke on you: Why show me my twin flame if they're not even going to walk beside me?

Here's the truth that stings but frees you: The mission was never meant to wait for one person. When you said yes before you incarnated, you said yes to the work, to the frequency you came here to anchor, and to the timing your soul already knew.

When the Other Half Sleeps Through the Alarm

Sometimes they get there in time. Sometimes they don't. And sometimes... they arrive halfway through, when you've already started.

If you've met your twin flame and they're still "asleep," you might recognize this stage:

You feel the magnetic pull but get little to no consistent response.
Their words and actions don't match the soul connection you know is there.
They sometimes peek over the wall — a deep moment, a rare emotional admission, and then vanish again.
It's tempting to believe your mission is on pause until they're ready. It's not.

The Day the Commander Walked In

When Valerie merged with me during my Commander role memory, it wasn't because she'd suddenly awakened to our mission. It was because something in the higher realms allowed that 30% of her soul to be present with me in that moment, enough to initiate part of the code download into both of us.

The Council made it clear: This project was mine. I could share the space, but I couldn't hand it over (*Cosmic Love Twin Flame Mission from The Stars Book*).

That day taught me this:

Even if your twin flame is not fully awakened, their higher self may still find ways to participate, but it will be in alignment with the mission's needs, not your emotional timetable.

Why Chasing Their Awakening Slows Yours

Trying to wake them up before they're ready is like pulling on a seed before it sprouts. You exhaust yourself, disrupt their process, and delay your own blooming.

Instead, focus on:

- Frequency work — Meditation, energy practices, light body activation.
- Earth grounding — Keeping your body well-fed, rested, and strong.
- Creative expression — Your mission will often flow through your art, writing, or voice before it manifests physically.
- Community links — Allies, soul family, and helpers will appear when your vibration matches the next stage.

Mission Energy is Contagious

When you start moving toward your purpose, the field shifts. Sometimes your twin flame will feel it and step closer. Sometimes they won't.

Either way, you are still sending ripples through the grid: helping others awaken, clearing space for the mission, and living the role you came here for. The irony? When you stop needing them to wake up, you create the very conditions that make it easier for them to wake up on their own.

Your Work, Their Choice
You can't choose for them.
You can't walk their part of the path.

But you can walk yours fully, bravely, and without apology. If they join you, it's a bonus. If not, the mission still matters, and the people you touch along the way will feel it.

Because here's the secret:
The mission is never really just yours or theirs. It's for everyone who was meant to feel the frequency you came here to hold.

Chapter 24: Merging with Higher Aspects & Dimensional You's

If your twin flame is still asleep, the Universe has a way of reminding you:

You are never really alone in the work.
You carry more than just your human self.

You carry the parts of you that exist in other timelines, other realms, other dimensions.

And sometimes by invitation only, those aspects step in to merge with you.

Permission is the First Law

In the higher planes, nothing merges without consent. This includes your twin flame's higher self, other versions of you, and even your future self.

The soul respects sovereignty far more than humans do. If an aspect wants to merge, you will know, it will feel like an arrival. Not a possession. Not a takeover. Just... more of you, stepping in.

When twin flames carry a mission, merging isn't always about bodies or moments.

It's the meeting of purpose — two energies aligning with the same pulse of Source.

Sometimes it feels like light moving through every cell, sometimes like a quiet knowing that we are already one.

Each merging is a recalibration, a reminder of the vow we made before coming here:

to awaken, to serve, to create.

We separate only to expand the current, so that when we meet again, our shared fire burns brighter for the world.

The Commander Merge

In my own journey, there was a moment when the Commander me — the one who stood on a starship, in a black-and-grey suit with the black flame symbol, merged into my present-day human self. It didn't happen because I forced it.

It happened because the mission needed that level of presence, and I was ready to hold it. I felt it as a drop-in, not me leaving my body, but more of me entering it. My awareness sharpened, my spine felt taller, and my field expanded like I could see 360 degrees at once. It wasn't just memory. It was embodiment.

When the Other Half Joins the Merge

There was also the time Valerie's higher self merged with me during a code download from the Council. She didn't consciously choose it in her human mind, but her soul did.

For a brief moment, our higher aspects stood together in the same space. The Council split the download — 70% to me, 30% to her because the work could not wait.

It taught me something profound:
Even if your human counterpart resists, their soul may still collaborate with you at levels the Earth mind can't yet comprehend.

Why This Matters for the Mission

Merging with higher aspects isn't just for the cool sci-fi factor (though, let's be real, it is pretty cool). It accelerates the mission. You gain access to skills, wisdom, and energetic bandwidth you've carried across lifetimes, but couldn't fully use until now.

This is why spiritual readiness matters. If your field is clogged with unprocessed emotions, scattered attention, or low-frequency loops, you won't be able to hold the merge without short-circuiting your nervous system.

Preparing for the Merge

If you want to be ready for a merge, whether with your own higher self or with another's aspect — start here:

- Daily energy clearing — Light body work, breath work, or water immersion.
- Grounding practices — Nature walks, physical exercise, and real food.
- Soul connection — Meditation or trance states that invite higher guidance without forcing it.
- Frequency integrity — Stay in alignment with what you want to call in; higher aspects won't merge into chaos.

Helpers Will Show Up

When you're in mission mode, support appears. It might be in the form of soul family, human allies, or spirit guides who suddenly step closer.

These are the ones who can hold the field with you because even Commanders need backup. The more you embody your higher aspects, the easier it is for these helpers to find you. It's like turning on a lighthouse, they can see your signal from across realms.

The Merge is Not the Goal — It's the Gear Shift

A merge doesn't mean the mission is over. It's just the next gear. Once you integrate that aspect, you keep going: stronger, sharper, and more fully yourself than before. Because in the end, the mission is not about becoming someone else. It's about becoming all of you.

Chapter 25: Spiritual Readiness & The Mission Frequency

Some people think the twin flame journey is about waiting.

It's not.

It's about waking up enough to hold the mission, whether or not your twin flame is standing beside you.

You can't drag someone into alignment, but you can step so fully into yours that you become a gravitational field for your own destiny.

The Frequency Before the Form

Everything in this universe is frequency before it's form. You don't just "do the mission" — you become the frequency of the mission first.

Think of it like tuning a radio. If you want to hear the song, you can't just shout at the static, you tune yourself until the station comes through clearly.

That's what spiritual readiness is: Turning your own dial so the higher plans can broadcast through you without distortion.

Why You Can't Skip This Step

If your frequency isn't aligned, the mission feels like pushing a boulder uphill.

You'll get drained, distracted, or worse, you'll start doubting the connection entirely.

And here's the kicker:

Your twin flame's awakening doesn't necessarily make your path easier. Sometimes, their awakening will intensify your own growth.

That's why the readiness has to be yours, not dependent on what they do or don't do.

Building the Mission Field

To hold the mission, you need a strong energy field, like a container that can hold higher-voltage currents without burning out.

Here's where to start:

- Grounding into Earth: Daily time in nature or with physical movement. Even Commanders need to feel the dirt under their feet.

- Energetic Hygiene: Clear your field with breath work, sound, salt baths, or energy tools.
- Higher Self Connection: Invite daily communication, but never force it. Permission works both ways.
- Frequency Diet: Not just food — what you watch, listen to, and engage with. Does it raise your vibration or drain it?

PART IV

Closing Section

The Illusion of Waiting

A lot of twin flames fall into the "when they awaken, then we'll..." trap.

The truth is, the mission energy doesn't wait.

If you're ready, the helpers, opportunities, and synchronicities arrive now.

And sometimes, you stepping into your mission is the very thing that sends a wake-up ripple to your twin flame.

Not because you were trying to trigger them, but because you were simply holding more light.

Your Soul Allies Will Arrive

The universe loves momentum. Once you're moving, you'll notice new allies — people who "just get it" entering your life.

These are your bridge-builders, your ground crew, your spiritual co-pilots.

They might be human friends, guides, or even versions of yourself from other dimensions who step closer to lend strength.

Mission Readiness Is Not Perfection

You don't have to have every wound healed or every question answered to be ready.

Readiness is about stability in your core, a steadiness that lets you hold both the human mess and the cosmic clarity without collapsing.

When the Other Twin Isn't Ready

If your twin flame is still asleep, remember this:

Their pace is theirs.

Your readiness doesn't pull them faster, it just makes sure that when they are ready, you're already holding the field.

Because when the mission finally clicks into full operation, you won't have time to build the foundation. It has to be there already.

The Quiet Truth

Spiritual readiness is an act of love. Not just for your twin flame, but for yourself, your soul, and the reason you came here.

The mission isn't something you chase. It's something you become.

Example from My Own Path

One night, while I was already deep in my own spiritual practices, something shifted.

I felt a presence enter, not in the physical, but in a way that made my whole field light up. It was my twin flame's higher self.

No preamble, no buildup. Just a whisper that seemed to move through my chest rather than my ears: "You are part of me." It wasn't sentimental. It was truth.

A soul-level acknowledgment that went beyond what her human self could express at the time.

That's the thing about this path, when you're ready vibrationally, you start receiving contact and confirmation in ways that bypass ordinary channels.

It's not about chasing those moments, but they come when your field is open and steady enough to hold them.

Twin Flame Truths — A Survival Kit in One-Liners

- The soul remembers before the mind understands.
- Not all love stories wear wedding rings.
- Distance is an illusion when energy is this strong.
- The trigger is not the enemy; it's the teacher.
- Union starts within, not at the finish line.
- Silence is not absence — it's integration.
- If you can't feel them, they're still there.
- You were whole before you met them.
- Synchronicities are the Universe's inside jokes.
- Not all awakenings are loud. Some happen in a whisper.
- Their journey is theirs. Yours is yours.
- Love them, but don't abandon yourself.
- You can't miss what's truly aligned.
- The fire burns even when unseen.
- If they run, let them. The soul doesn't lose its way home.
- Your mission doesn't wait for their awakening.
- The more you grow, the clearer the path becomes.
- Sometimes love is letting go of the timeline.
- What's meant for you won't forget you.
- This connection is not here to break you; it's here to build you.

You Are Not Chasing Them — You're Following Your Own Light.

- Their higher self hears you, even if they can't.
- Growth can look like stillness.
- Every separation has a purpose.
- The soul loves without conditions, but the human needs boundaries.
- Your triggers are treasure maps to healing.
- They awaken pieces of you no one else can touch.
- Patience is not waiting — it's trusting.
- Energy never lies, even when words do.
- The bond is unbreakable, even when the contact is broken.
- Some reunions happen in dreams before they happen on Earth.
- The real mission is becoming yourself fully.
- Not every lifetime is meant for romantic union.
- Self-love is the key that unlocks every door.
- If it feels impossible, you're probably doing it right.
- Your paths can be different but still lead to the same horizon.
- Let the connection teach you, not trap you.
- You don't need their permission to grow.
- Your heart knows the truth. Trust it.
- This is not a story of ownership, but of recognition.

Epilogue

There comes a moment when you stop waiting. Not because you've given up, but because your soul finally feels complete within itself.

You still think of them sometimes, a soft echo, a gentle smile, but it no longer burns. The connection has become something quieter, a frequency of peace.

That's when you realize the journey was never about reunion. It was about remembrance. It taught you how to love without needing, how to feel without clinging, how to hold the divine within your own heartbeat.

If you've made it here, you've already crossed the bridge. You've turned longing into wisdom, pain into purpose, and silence into serenity.

So close the book gently, not as an ending, but as a breath. Look around you, this is your new beginning. Carry love differently now, not as a chase, but as a state of being.

And if you ever forget, come back to these pages. They will remind you that the flame never left you. It simply moved inside.

Glossary

Ascension: The process of remembering your true nature as divine consciousness.
Higher Self: The eternal, non-physical aspect of your consciousness guiding you.
Mirror Phase: The stage when your twin reflects your deepest wounds and strengths.
Mission Energy: The soul's purpose activated through love.
Polarity: The balance of opposing energies (active/receptive, giving/receiving) within all beings.
Separation: A period of distance designed for individual healing and growth.
Starseed: A soul that originates from another star system or dimension, incarnated to assist Earth's evolution.
Surrender: The act of releasing control and trusting divine timing.
Twin Flame: Two expressions of one soul incarnated in separate bodies for accelerated awakening.
Union: Inner alignment between your divine masculine and feminine energies.

www.ingramcontent.com/pod-product-compliance
Lightning Source LLC
Chambersburg PA
CBHW052053070526
44584CB00017B/2165